Introduction

Not all items in this book are depression glass, if you mean by the term machine made tank glass. Many of these items were not machine made, nor are they tank glass. Many are of pot glass quality. All items in this book are, however, depression era production, some falling as early as 1920, others not until 1940-50. The later items are included as they have appearance of being made in the 1920-40 period and are thus collected as such. They are now collectibles in their own right even though they lack age. Originally, depression glass was a term applied only to "machine made tank glass." Today collectors have expanded to include many types of glassware, both as to pattern and origin.

COVER

Items on front cover, from top down, left to right.

Houze Glass Company, two tone jade electric lamp.

Consolidated Lamp and Glass Company, *Dogwood* 11" vase, crystal frost.

Indiana, *Fluted Colonial* sugar bowl.

Banded *Aurora* comport, crystal ice, satin iridescent.

Melon Rib creamer, jade green, Fenton Art Glass Company.

U.S. Glass Company, *Cumula* pattern, green cloud decoration on iridescent glass.

L. E. Smith, white opal swan dish or candy dish.

English Hobnail, No. 555, Westmoreland Glass company, green.

Fancy Square sandwich server, jade green, Co-operative Flint Glass Company.

No. 18, low square candlestick, green, U.S. Glass.

Sunset Line, *Orchid* pattern pin tray, U.S. Glass.

Plate 1

A 1928 catalog gave this full page spread to its 1928 beauties. The No. 2549 is *Imperial's No. 682-Pillar Flute. No. 682-Pillar Flute* was made in 30 known items, in iridescent, imperial green, Rose-Marie, crystal, and possibly other Imperial colors. No. 2476 and No. 2475 vases are crystal glass with fired-on colors. The *Flaming Poppy* and the *American Beauty Rose* vases are only two of the many vase lines offered in fired-on colors during the late 1920s through the early 1930s.

FROSTED BLOCK. 1928-1930s. Imperial. During *Frosted Block's* long production, transparent colors were Rose-Marie, imperial green, blue, amber and crystal; the sea-foam colors (transparent color with opalescent edge) were Harding Blue, Moss Green and Burnt Almond. Shown is Rose-Marie.

FLUTED SWIRL VASE. Another Imperial product in iridescent and transparent colors, imperial green, Rose-Marie, crystal.

FLORAL AND DIAMOND BAND. 1927-early 1930s. Transparent jade green, pink and iridescent. U.S. Glass Company catalogs reveal an entire set identical to the mold shapes of *Floral* and *Diamond Band,* void of all pattern.

FANCY GLASSWARE IN GORGEOUS COLORS

No. 2549 — 35¢
Golden iridescent glass in fluted pattern. Reflects all the rich sparkling colors of the rainbow. Big 5½-inch size.

No. 2476 — 20¢
Iridescent Footed Bowl
For serving mayonnaise, preserves, nuts, etc.

No. 2550 — 35¢
New Cut Glass Pattern — Two Strong Handles
Rose Marie Double Handled Fancy Dish
Glassware with the rosy glow of dawn. The rose color is right in the glass—will never wash or wear off. Glittering new cut glass pattern. A double handled fancy dish suitable for serving candy, jelly, pickles, etc. Measures 4⅜ inches across top; 6⅝ inches wide including handles.

Flaming Poppy Vase — **High Raised Design**
Flaming red poppy and harmonious green leaves stand out in extra high raised relief from the surface. Raised lattice design covers golden finish glass vase. Very ornamental. Gorgeous coloring that pleases the eye. Full 6 inches high.

No. 2475 — 40¢
High Raised American Beauty Vase
Coral pink colored glass in all-over lattice design decorated with large American Beauty rose and harmonious green leaves standing out in high raised relief. Large massive size—measures 7½ inches high. A pretty gift.

No. 255 — 45¢
Rose Marie — **Square Plate**
Glassware with the rosy glow of dawn. The rose color is right in the glass—will never wash or wear off. Glittering new cut glass pattern. For sandwiches, salads, pie, etc. Large, useful 7¾-inch size.

No. 2552 — 35¢
Fluted Iridescent Vase
Beautiful golden iridescent glass in dainty spiral fluted pattern. All the rich colors of the rainbow sparkle and glisten from the golden surface of this beautiful vase. Tall enough for long stemmed flowers—7½ inches high.

No. 2501 — 85¢
Set of 6 Jade Green Glass Tumblers
The very newest idea in glassware. Beautiful new cut glass floral design. The rich green color is right in the glass—will never wash or wear off. Full size for family use.

No. 2502 — 35¢
Jade Green Glass Footed Jelly Dish
The very newest idea in glassware. The rich green color is right in the glass—will never wash or wear off. Can be used for jelly, jam or relishes, etc., etc. Beautiful new cut glass floral design. Strong stem with wide base to prevent upsetting. Very ornamental. 4¾ inches wide; 4½ inches high.

Plate 2

HOLLOW HEAD HORSE BOOKENDS. 1938-42. Crystal and yellowish crystal. Origin unknown. Many glasshouses made horse bookends and all are similar. ROW I, 1 and 2. 5½" high, crystal.

DUNCAN NOVELTY SWANS. Duncan & Miller. 1943 on. Crystal, ruby, avocado, chartreuse, teakwood, opalescents and biscayne green. Duncan issued the swans until U.S. Glass purchased the Duncan & Miller plant in 1955. Thereafter U.S. Glass has periodically issued the swans in crystal, citron green and copen blue. ROW I 3, chartreuse 7-1/8" swan candleholder. 1949. ROW I 4, crystal 7" long swan dish. 1943.

CRYSTAL PIGGY JAR BANK. After 1930. Owens-Illinois, Crystal, fired-on gold, red and black. A packaging jar for food products. ROW II 1, piggy jar bank, 7-1/2".

FIGURAL POWDER JARS. Jeannette, 1938-42. Crystal and iridescent. Sold to five-and-dime syndicates, and to packaging houses for beauty and bath products. Sold as powder jars, candy jars and bath jars. ROW II 2 and 3, rear and front view, Scottie dog, iridescent; ROW II 5, donkey, black cover insert, inscribed "Bowl o' Beauty Co., Maywood, Ill.", crystal; ROW III 3, elephant, crystal; ROW III 4 and 5, crystal deer, iridescent deer.

COVERED DUCK BOXES. Crystal and iridescent. 1938-42. ROW III 1, covered duck box, iridescent fired-on yellow bill; ROW III 2, covered duck box, iridescent plain, each 6" long, 4-1/2" high to top of head.

HOLLOW MADONNA. Crystal, origin unknown. Several glasshouses made madonna figurals. Their catalog illustrations appear strikingly similar. This madonna is three mold, heavy, hollow, and bubbles are in the glass. ROW II 4, crystal hollow madonna 6" high.

OWL FLOWER BLOCKS 1928, origin unknown. Amber, rose and green. The 4-1/2" owl flower blocks matched a tiered optic console bowl. ROW IV 1 and 2, Green and amber owl flower block, 4-1/2" high.

CAMEL. Crystal, 1928, origin unknown. Advertised as card or cigarette holder. ROW IV 3, crystal camel, 7-1/2" long.

SWAN DISH. L.E. Smith. 1943-19____. Crystal and frost. Today cast in black, white opal, transparent and frosted blue, and advertised as soap dishes. ROW IV 4, swan dish, crystal frost, 8" long, 4-1/2" high.

Plate 3

CRUCIFIX CANDLEHOLDER. Origin unknown. 1911-1920s. Crystal, white opal. Many factories, including but not limited to L. E. Smith, Westmoreland, U.S. Glass, Canton, McKee, Cambridge and others made a crucifix candleholder. ROW I 1, crucifix white opal candleholder 9-3/8" high.

DOLPHIN CONSOLE CANDLEHOLDERS. Westmoreland. 1925. Crystal, amber, green, blue, white opal. 1940 to date, white opal and black. The dolphin motif is on a small Westmoreland line, comports, bowls, lamps, center handle sandwich server. ROW I 2 and 3, dolphin console candleholders, 9-1/4" high, white opal.

CAMBRIDGE GOBLER. Cambridge, 1930. Crystal, black. A novelty product in the Cambridge animal line. ROW I 4, Cambridge gobler candy jar, crystal.

RABBIT MOLD. British made. Crystal. Imported during the depression era. ROW II 1. Crystal, 7-3/4" long.

DANCING GIRL. U.S. Glass, 1927. Crystal, apple-green, rose-pink, sky-blue, satin colors. Sold in vanity sets of two colognes and one puff box. ROW II 2, crystal dancing girl puff box.

DUCK ASHTRAY. Duncan and Miller. 1943. Crystal, ruby, chartreuse, biscayne green. Duncan's Duck Line—solid ducks, assorted ashtray ducks, and covered duck dishes (two-piece duck with cover). ROW II 3, crystal 5" duck ashtray.

LUCKY JOE BANK. Patent 112688-6. Crystal, fired on red color accents. A packaging jar for Nash's Prepared Mustard. ROW II 4, crystal Lucky Joe bank.

ELEPHANT FAMILY. Origin unknown. Crystal. Elephant mother and two babies powder jar, lid only shown. ROW II 4, elephant family powder jar lid 4-7/8" diameter, crystal.

HEN ON STRAW NEST. Origin unknown. Crystal, white opal. 1915-40s. Advertised in 1934 as utility dishes and in 1941 as novelty dishes. Many factories made hens of assorted sizes, detail and nest variants. Hens from many factories are still reissued today. ROW III 1, hen on straw nest, crystal.

COVERED SWAN. Origin unknown. Crystal and crystal frost. Late 1920s. ROW III 2, crystal frost swan dish, painted eye, 7" long.

APPLES-IN-BASKET. 1920s. Origin unknown. White opal, fired on colors. Base is white opal, lid is crystal with color fired on. ROW III 3, apples-in-basket novelty box, 4-1/8" diameter.

HOUND PUP. 1955, origin unknown. Crystal, flashed red or blue on crystal, amber. Two sizes, 3" high, and 2-3/4" high. ROW III 4 and 5. Crystal hound pup. Refer to candy container books.

CHICKEN-ON-THE-NEST. J. H. Millstein Co. 1946. Crystal, fired on yellow nest, red comb. ROW IV 1 and 2, chicken-on-the-nest in crystal, and fired on colors.

BLACK GLASS HENS. 1920s-30s. Rare. Black and white hen sets on basket weave base, other hen sets on checkerboard type base. ROW IV 3, all black hen 5-1/2" long; ROW IV 4, black and white opal hen, 5-1/4" long.

SCOTTIE DOG, HEAD UP. J. S. Crosett Co. 1946. Crystal. Scottie dog, head down, not shown, is variant. Both candy containers named by candy container authors. ROW IV 5.

Plate 4

MODERNE CLASSIC PATTERN. Indiana, 1928-34. Yellow and white or green and white, both with platinum trim; crystal, pink, green in plain or etched pattern (advertised under different pattern names). Indiana advertisements stated "*Moderne Classic* embraces all the pieces the public will ever want, including . . . relish dishes, comports, cake stands, rose bowls, mayonnaise sets, sugars and creams, candy boxes, cheese dishes, etc." Item 1 is a different motif advertised in the *Moderne Classic* assortment. ROW I 1: *Moderne Classic* two-handled cake tray 10-1/4"; ROW I 2, 7-1/4" plate; ROW I 3, 4-1/2" diameter, 4" high candleholder; ROW I 4 and 5, sugar and cream; ROW I 6, 5-1/2" mayonnaise bowl, octagon rim, handles.

BUBBLE FOOT STEMWARE. Anchor Hocking, 1938-19__. Royal ruby, forest green bowls with crystal feet. Crystal stemware was made in *Cut No. 411-Laurel,* a band of connected leaves. Open stock stemware has been sold to date, except for *Laurel Cut No. 411* which has not been reissued. Montgomery Ward in late 1960 sold stemware in their old gold amber color to match the old gold Sandwich line. Anchor Hocking issued two styles of bubble feet, both shown here. ROW II 1, Bubble foot, 15 oz., 5-1/2" high ice tea, forest green; ROW II 2, Royal Ruby 6 oz., 3-3/4" high sherbet, bubble foot; ROW III 1, forest green swirled bubble foot 5-7/8" high goblet; ROW III 2, forest green 9 oz., 4-1/2" high goblet, bubble foot.

HERITAGE. Federal. 1940-1960, crystal. Berry sets made in crystal, pink, spring green, madonna blue. Only occasional items made after 1940. Original 1940 packing box lists starter set as cups, saucers, 9-1/2" plates. Plates actually measure 9-1/4". This was a small line of 11 items. ROW II 3, crystal *Heritage* creamer; ROW II 4, 5" sauce dish; ROW II 5, 8" salad plate; ROW II 6, cup and saucer set; ROW II 7, sugar.

SERRATED EDGE NOVELTY COMPORT. Finished product of Rank M. Whiting & Co. line No. 2074. Emerald green, sterling base. ROW III 3, serrated edge novelty comport 5-1/2" high.

FROSTED LEAF BOX. 1928. Satin frost colors, crystal, pink, green. Leaf design on cover, tiered three-toed base. ROW III 4, box, satin frost green, 4-5/8" diameter, 5" high.

L. E. SMITH SWAN DISH. L. E. Smith, 1928-19—. White opal, black jet, plain or fired-on orange eyes, beak. Made today in white opal and Smith's frosted colors. Most animal open and covered items were advertised as "dishes." Swan dishes were made in several sizes, the largest shown here, also decorated in silver overlay. ROW III 5, dish 5-3/4" high, 8-1/2" long.

ORNATE CANDLEHOLDERS. Lotus purchased handmade finished glassware from many U.S. factories to decorate, selling the finished product under their label. ROW IV 1 and 3, cobalt 4-1/2" base diameter, fancy candleholders, floral silver overlay. Lotus Decoration No. 65.

OPENWORK SANDWICH TRAY. Imperial, 1931. Imperial states this sandwich tray is theirs. It is not illustrated in any of their remaining records,

but they did many openwork edge pieces during this time. ROW IV 2, sandwich tray, 10-1/4" diameter.

DOUBLE SHIELD. L. E. Smith. Cobalt, white opal, black jet, pink, plain or decorated in silver overlay. Smith lists this as No. 600 in the catalogs. ROW IV 4. No. 600 candleholder, cobalt 5-7/8" long.

Plate 5

NORTHWOOD'S HEXAGON CANDLESTICK in Chinese Coral, stands 8-1/2" tall, 4-1/2" base diameter. H. Northwood Glass Company 1922. ROW I 1.

PANELED OVOID CANDY JAR BASE. Mandarin Red, 1930-35. 4-1/4" rim diameter, stands 10-1/2" tall with lid. Fenton Art Glass Company, 1928-1930s. ROW I 2.

DOLPHIN HANDLED ovoid candy jar. Fenton Glass Company. 9-1/4" tall, 4" rim diameter. ROW I 3.

FENTON'S NUMBER 449 candlestick. 8-1/2" tall. Fenton issued an identical stick 10" tall, referred to as number 349. Shown here in Mandarin Red. ROW I 4.

FLARED BOWL. Footed console bowl issued by N. Northwood Glass Company 1922-24. This bowl also made with advertising in raised relief, "Dollar Savings and Trust Wheeling West Virginia." This bowl stands 4-1/2" high, 10" rim diameter, is shown in Chinese Red with jet foot. The bowl was also issued in a moonstone color, referred to as opal, on the foot only, with choice of colors for the bowl. ROW II 1. H. Northwood got much of its financing from the Dollar Savings and Trust, which was ultimately to buy the business to re-sell, trying to recapture the sums granted through loans for operating costs.

FANCY FLUTE candlestick. Fenton Art Glass Company, Mandarin Red. Saucer is 5" diameter, stands 2-1/4" tall. ROW II 2.

ROLLED RIM BOWL. This bowl is 8-3/4" diameter, stands 3-1/2" high, in Chinese Red. H. Northwood product; however Fenton also made a similar bowl. ROW II 3.

TRUMPET CANDLESTICK. Diamond Glass-Ware Company, 6-1/4" tall, 4" base diameter. The shaft is solid, the flared trumpet end hollow to the shaft. Olive green jade. ROW III 1.

WIDE SWIRL bowls. ROW III 2, ROW IV 2. The wide swirl bowls have matching candlesticks as shown (the Trumpet Swirl Candlesticks). Both bowls were issued by the Diamond Glass-Ware Company. The possibility also exists that they were issued by H. Northwood, since the molds, management and equipment were being shuffled around in the change-over of the Northwood Plant in Indiana, Penna., to the Dugan Glass Works, and ultimately to the Diamond Glass-Ware Company. The bowls have been documented in several shapes and sizes. Top bowl shown in Chinese Red stands 2-1/4" high, with a rim diameter of 10-1/4". Lower bowl shown in olive green jade, stands 3-1/2" high, 11-1/2" rim diameter.

DOLPHIN HANDLED bonbon. ROW III 3. This is a favorite shape in the satin iridescent line of Fenton, and has been noted in several of the jade colors. Shown in green jade, bonbon stands 4-1/2" high, 6-3/4" rim

diameter. The item appeared in 1928 trade catalogs continuing into the 1930s.

SWIRLED TRUMPET candlesticks. ROW IV 1 and 3. The candlesticks will be found in most of the H. Northwood jade and satin iridescent colors. Candlesticks, 6-1/4" high, with base diameter of 4".

All items courtesy Cheryl Leaf Antiques, Bellingham, Washington. Photography Floyd W. Wear Studio, Blaine, Washington.

Plate 6

JADES. ROW I 1, handled candleholder, Houze Glass Company. Electrical fixture and shade tranforms this candleholder into a lamp. Nile green, Jadine, Coralex, Veined Onyx, black jade. ROW I 2, tall comport, origin unknown. It is known that both Diamond and Northwood poured this jade color. Fenton did not. 7-1/2" high, 6-5/8" diameter. ROW I 3, flared rim bowl, 3-1/2" high, 8-7/8" diameter; made in all of Fenton's jade and most Florentine colors. ROW I 4, two tone jade lamp, Houze Glass Company, Jadine and black jade; four pieces of jade glassware connected together for electric fixture, paper stick trademark. ROW I 5, jade electric lamp, square base, origin unknown.

ROW II 1, lemon server, Fenton; jade and Florentine colors. ROW II 2, fan vase, Fenton, jade and Florentine colors. ROW II 4, tumbler, origin unknown, jade green, 5-1/4" high. ROW II 5, tumbler, Co-operative Flint, Fancy Square pattern, black foot 5-1/4" high. ROW II 6, Fancy Square 7-3/8" jade green plate. ROW II 7, footed creamer, jade green. ROW II 8, Fancy Square saucer, jade green.

ROW III 1, rolled rim bowl, Northwood circle, all jade colors; shown in Northwood jade, 3" high, 9-1/2" diameter. ROW III 3, basket vase, Fenton, jade and Florentine colors, 6" high, 8-1/2" diameter, metal bail. ROW III 5, flared comport, footed. Origin unknown. Olive green jade, 4-1/2" high, 9-1/4" diameter.

ROW IV 1, melon rib creamer, Fenton, jade and Florentine colors. ROW IV 2, 3, 4, Lotus. Fenton, jade and Florentine colors. Candleholders 1-3/4" high. Console bowl 8-7/8" diameter, 3-1/2" high. ROW IV 5. Fenton panel rose bowl, jades and Florentine colors.

NON-JADE TRANSPARENT GLASS. ROW II 3, crystal coal scuttle, New Martinsville Glass Co. ROW III 2, *Swirled Dolphin* candleholder, L. E. Smith-Greensburg Glass Companies, crystal, pink, green, amber and black. ROW III 4, low *No. 18-U.S.* candleholder, U.S. Glass, 1920s-30s. Bright transparents and satin finish colors, crystal, sky-blue, apple green (shown), amber, rose-pink, black. Low No. 18 candleholders were advertised to accompany U.S. Glass low window box, similar to Smith's *Snake Dance* window box shown elsewhere.

OCTAGON PLATE, Fenton, 6, 7, and 8" plates, jade green.

DIAMOND OPTIC small handled basket, Fenton, jade green. Note hob for wire bail handle. Also made with small dolphin glass handles. (Photography by *Merle Brown, Brown's Commercial Photography, Spokane, Wash.*)

Plate 7

JADES. All pieces made by Fenton Art Glass Company, also made in Fenton's Florentine finish, lustre colors and other jade colors.

NO. 6252 candlestick, Fenton, Mongolian green (deeper shade than jade green). The wafer on the end shaft of the stick is the only apparent difference in Fenton's No. 449 and No. 349 candlestick shapes.

LOOP HANDLE sandwich server, Fenton, jade green.

FANCY SQUARE sandwich plate, Co-operative Flint. Introduced in 1929 in shiny pot glass colors, crystal, ruby, cobalt, amber, aquamarine blue, green, rose, and jade-ebony, jade green. Notice the difference between Fenton's jade green and Co-operative Flint's jade green.

EIGHT SPINE PILLOW MOLD, footed, rolled edge console bowl. Usually 9-10" diameter. Fenton, jade green, 1928-35.

EMBOSSED ROSE powder jar. Made by Lancaster or Hocking Glass Co. (both run by same company officials in same city, different plant managers). Long tapered cone cover has a spray of roses, leaves, stem. Jade green.

8" ROUND PLATE, Fenton, jade green.

CYLINDER candlesticks, Fenton, Mandarin yellow jade.

ALMOND CUP, Fenton, jade green.

ROCKING HORSE ink blotter. Mandarin yellow, not made in satin iridescent or lustre colors.

TAPERED STEM candlestick, Fenton, jade green. The tapered stem is hidden by the position of the camera.

JADES, 1922-35. Jade glass is an opaque glass with a slick feel, resembling Chinese jade stone. We most often think of jade as being green but it is not necessarily so. Mandarin Red, Mandarin Yellow, Mongolian Green, Jade, and Flame are Fenton's color names. Chinese Red, Chinese Yellow, Jade, and Blue are H. Northwood's names. Turkey Red and Chinese Blue are names applied by yet another glass house. The U.S. Glass Company promoted their jade line under the name of CARRARA WARE, and used color names such as Coral, Jade, Pearl Gray, Chinese Yellow. The Imperial Glass Company is not known to have issued any jade ware.

There appears to be no difference in composition of the various colors, except for a few colors such as Fenton's turquoise which is unlike any other company's ware. The jades were sometimes crizzled with faint iridescence. Only the ivory, blue and green jades have been verified in this crizzled effect. All firms used company color names. However, after the item leaves the manufacturing house, being sold to a jobber or retail outlet, the factory color names are often lost. One example was Sears Roebuck Company, which used its "Harmony House" color names.

Jades are different from their transparent sisters in that the color is opaque. The name "jade glass" is derived only from the likeness to jade, and not from any certain chemical composition.

Satin iridescents and lustre colors were also used with the same blanks as many of the jade items. Fenton's satin iridescent (stretch) is called "Florentine"; Imperial's line is called Satin Iridescents; U.S. Glass refers to its satin iridescent line as Aurora. In the line are different colors with individual pattern names. In each case, the glassware is what collectors refer to as Stretch Glassware today. Stretch glass is not the same as the lustre line companies made from the same molds. Lustre is a slick, shiny, mineral finish, usually in marigold colors. Satin iridescents are a satin stretched somewhat rough, never slick and shiny to the touch.

Plate 8

1929 advertisements list these as *Marguerite Cut* or *Spray Cut*. All items shown are in pink, but they were made in green also.

A. *Cubist II.* Berry bowl set, a thinner, lighter glassware than in *Cubist* pattern. Bowl 7-1/4", sauce dishes 4-1/2".

B. Spray bud vase, 9-3/4" high.

C. Marguerite night set, bottle 6" high, 16 oz.; tumbler 3" high.

D. Castor set, Marguerite, handled stand, pair 3" shakers, aluminum tops.

E. Butter tub, 4-1/4" diameter, 1" deep, Marguerite.

F. Bonbon dish, 7-1/2" octagonal, Marguerite.

G. Jelly dish, 7-1/2" diameter, Marguerite.

H. Cake plate, 10" diameter, two large open handles, Marguerite.

I. Salad Bowl, 9" diameter, 2-1/2" deep, Marguerite.

J. Mayonnaise set, flared bowl, 6-1/2" diameter, glass ladle with cutting on bowl, Marguerite.

K. Salt, pepper shakers, 4-1/2" high Spray, nickel-plated tops.

L. Candy box, 5" diameter, 6-1/2" high including cover, Marguerite.

M. Pickle dish, oval 6-1/2" long, 3-3/4" wide, Marguerite.

N. Console set, no cutting, flared bowl 12" diameter, pair of 4-1/2" ruffled candlesticks, 4" flower block. Console bowl is paneled optic, candleholders slightly ruffled.

Most items shown are of Imperial Glass origin. It is not known if Imperial also cut their blanks or if another decorating concern cut the motifs and applied the same motif to several companies' blanks.

GLASSWARE CHARMING IN PINK

Plate 9

VEINED ONYX. 1928-32. Occasional items were issued in this two-color effect, black with white veins. ROW I 1, veined onyx 9-1/4" plate; ROW I 2, 6-3/4" square comport.

INK ITEMS. New Martinsville and L. E. Smith have many ink items illustrated in their catalogs. Advertisements place these items between 1920-30. ROW I 3, ink holder for quill pen, 2-3/4" base diameter; ROW III 1, quill pen ink holder; ROW IV 2, oblong two-piece ink holder and pen rest.

SNAKE DANCE CRIMPED VASE. L. E. Smith 1928-32. Rich black, cobalt blue. Made for the Woolworth stores. ROW I 4, two-handled footed loving cup vase made in two sizes, the smaller shown here. The motif is girls dancing with snakes high in the air, and Pan playing his pipe. Also made without the snake dancers in plain glass with silver bands or silver floral decor

CAMBRIDGE SMALL COMPARTMENT TRAY. 1922-30. Black, blue, amber, green and peach. Advertised as a tray for cream-sugar and shakers and again as a tray for four bridge glasses. Trademarked within the triangle. ROW II 1, 7" handle to handle, black.

LACE RENAISSANCE. L. E. Smith 1928-35. Cobalt blue, black, pink, green, amber. Advertised as *Lace Renaissance* in wholesale catalogs. ROW II 2, cake plate, footed, 11-1/2" diameter, 3" high, black.

CAMBRIDGE CAKE-SANDWICH TRAY. 1922-34. Amber, emerald, mulberry, green, peach, blue, crystal, black, ruby. Typical Cambridge handle. There appears to be no difference in quality of the black glass made by the numerous glass houses. ROW II 3, server, black.

KIMBERLEY. U.S. Glass Co. 1926-28. Decorated on black, ruby glass. Console sets, flower bowls, candlesticks, candy boxes, cigarette boxes, dresser sets, etc., were decorated in Kimberly pattern. ROW III 2, Kimberly flared comport, 9-1/4" diameter, 5-3/4" high.

PYRAMID. New Martinsville. Late 1920, early 1930 period. Black, green, pink, and satin frost colors, pink and green. Protected by design patent. The creamer is handled, the sugar is not. ROW III 3, pyramid black sugar; ROW III 4, pyramid black creamer.

VORTEX TUMBLERS. Vortex made several sizes in tumblers with holes in base. These were used for paper cup liner inserts. ROW III 4, 10 oz. tumbler.

BANDED COMPORT. L. E. Smith 1928-32. Black, cobalt blue. ROW III 6, comport with gold bands, 3-1/2" high, 5-1/4" diameter, black.

SMITH FLOWER BLOCKS. 1925-35. Green, pink, amber, cobalt, crystal; black and frosted colors, pink, green, crystal frost. All the Smith vases had flower blocks to fit. ROW IV 1, black flower block, 4-3/8" diameter.

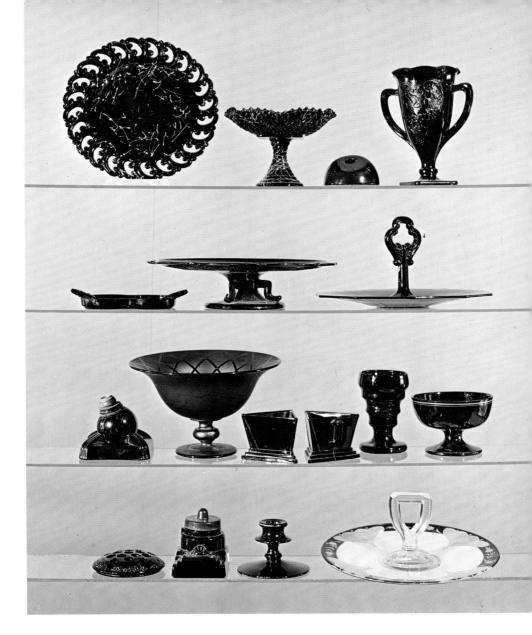

LOW CANDLESTICK. All depression era colors. This example of candlestick shown was made in varied detail by numerous glass factories, each factory adapting the design so as not to be identical. Low candlesticks of this design were advertised in 1920-1930. ROW III 3, low candlestick, black.

CUT BUTTERFLY SANDWICH SERVER. 1925. Fancy crystal with fired-on yellow, black decoration, then cut in *Butterfly* cutting, an elaborate "art glass" item of the time. ROW IV 4, sandwich server, 10-1/2" diameter.

Plate 10

PLAIN PLATONITE. Hazel Atlas, 1933-38. White opal. Platonite is not only white opal, but a durable, heat resistant glassware. Not all white opal is Platonite. The two tumblers are white opal, not Platonite, and sold in open stock. Hazel Atlas made plain round dinnerware from 1929-35 in black glass, green, some pink in the same molds. ROW I 1, Platonite 9" dinner plate; ROW I 2, Platonite cup-saucer set; ROW I 3, white opal open stock clown 5-1/8" tumbler, fired-on red, black, yellow; ROW I 4, white opal 4-3/4" table tumbler.

COLONIAL CANDLEHOLDERS. 1933-37. White opal, green, pink. Many candlesticks advertised as "Colonial Pattern" in catalogs. Handled candle-holders, not shown, made by New Martinsville. ROW I 5 and 6, Colonial white opal 4" high, 3-1/2" base candleholders.

OPALINE BASKET VASE. Ribbed vase in basket shape, applied gold on handles, decorated with green polkadots. ROW II 1, opaline basket vase, optional flower block.

JUBILEE. Lancaster, 1925-30. Topaz, green, pink. A Hocking showroom advertisement in trade journals listed this pattern as belonging to Lancaster glass, a subsidiary of Hocking. Another advertisement listed this as a product of Standard. The blank is Lancaster and perhaps Standard made the cutting. ROW II 2, topaz jubilee sugar; ROW II 3, creamer; ROW II 4, 6" saucer; ROW II 5, 7" plate.

PANSY FLOWER BOWL. Origin unknown. Late 1920s. Pink, green. Northwood, Fenton and others made thin blown flower novelty items. ROW III 1, *Pansy* flower bowl, green, 3-1/4" high, 5-3/4" diameter, optional flower block.

SMITH HOBNAIL FLOWER BOWLS. L. E. Smith. Late 1920s to 1940s. Cobalt blue, black, white opal, transparent pink-green. Smith re-issued some of their black line in the 1950s and periodically re-issue older molds to the present. ROW III 2, flower bowl, pink; ROW III 3, flower bowl, black. Both are 3-3/4" high, 5" diameter, flower blocks optional.

SAILBOAT ASHTRAY. Hazel Atlas, 1938. ROW IV 1, cobalt, metal sails affixed. Advertised in premium catalogs and open stock.

TRIPLE BAND BOWL with fired-on decoration. Late 1920s. Blue or orange fired-on crystal base glass, three black bands circling pattern. Small assortment made in occasional pieces. ROW IV 2, fired-on blue over crystal, black bands, 9-1/2".

PILLAR FLUTE TWIN CANDLEHOLDERS. Imperial, 1933-36. Rose-marie, green, crystal; white opal 1938-40s. Sold in *Pillar Flute* assortment in Imperial ads. This varies from *Pillar Flute* pattern in that the flutes swirl. ROW IV 3 and 4, 4-1/2" double socket candlesticks, green.

Plate 11

ENGLISH HOBNAIL 555. Westmoreland, 1924. Amber, green, roselin. This pattern has been re-issued to date in crystal, new frost colors of raspberry, peach, blue, pink. All roselin, green and amber are of earliest vintage. However, be careful not to mistake the new Golden Sunset amber for the older amber coloring. ROW I 1, 9-3/4" handled basket, green.

TIARA SANDWICH. 1970-197-. Indiana Glass. Ruby, Sandwich gold. Special order for Tiara exclusive, made from the old Indiana Sandwich molds. The Tiara line can only be obtained from the Tiara Jewelry Home Party Plans as gifts to the hostess. ROW I 2, gold goblet 5-1/2"; ROW I 3, gold cup; ROW I 4, salad plate 8-3/8"; ROW I 5, 10-1/4" dinner plate, Tiara Exclusive trade-sticker; ROW I 6, gold dome covered butter dish.

SUNSET LINE. U.S. Glass. 1924-27. The satin finish sunset line is red fading to yellow and often back to red. An assortment of U.S. patterns are cast in *Sunset*. ROW II 1, *Chatham* candy jar, 1/2 lb./8-3/4" high; ROW II 2, Colonial style Sunset sugar bowl, 6-3/4" handle to handle; *Orchid* pin tray, 7-1/2" oval.

DOLPHIN STEMWARE. Origin unknown. Green, pink dolphins, crystal bowl. The dolphins appear identical in size, shape to those made by Fenton. Verification has not been made. ROW II 4, green dolphin goblet; ROW II 5, wine.

PLEATED JADE-ITE. Anchor Hocking. Mid-1940-1964. Jade-ite color, Fire-King trademark. Brochure from factory states ". . . the new and only heat-proof glass dinnerware in the delicate beauty of green jade." Peach lustre, a carmel color, made in the late 1950s-early 1960s. ROW III 1, 9-1/8" dinner plate; ROW III 2, Coupe soup, 7-5/8", ROW III 3, 4-7/8" dessert; ROW III 4 and 5, cup and saucer set.

IRIS. Jeannette. Shown in Book I. Shown here only as an example of premium packaging. The metal lid is embossed, "Creamed Cottage Cheese." ROW III 6, 6" high. Iris tumbler, marigold lustre, metal embossed lid.

SUNRAY. Fostoria, 1935-40. Azure, amber, topaz, green, ruby, crystal. Advertised as *Sunburst Design* in 1936 catalog. ROW III 7, topaz 9 oz., 5-3/4" goblet; ROW III 8, amber 5-1/2 oz. sherbet.

CUMULA. U.S. Glass, 1922. Green cloud decoration on translucent iridized glass, as described in advertisements. ROW IV 1, 4-1/2" high comport, *Green cloud* decoration. Cumula was made in transparent colors, satin iridescent, lustre, green cloud, and sunset finish.

AZTEC BERRY BOWL. Federal. 1940-late. Amber, crystal. An unnamed berry bowl set in Federal catalogs listed only as A-8. Set consists of berry bowl, 7-3/4" diameter, and 4-1/2" dessert. ROW IV 2, berry bowl, amber.

OVAL ASHTRAY-COASTER COMBINATION. Maryland Glass Co. Cobalt blue. 1936-7. Spade, club, diamond and heart in stippled background border the ashtray-coaster combination. ROW IV 3, Maryland oval ashtray, cobalt blue.

LANCASTER-STANDARD CUTTING on creamer-sugar set 1925-30. Another floral, vertical line cut. ROW IV 4 and 5.

Plate 12

1929 CATALOG ADVERTISEMENT.

HAND PAINTED AZALEA GLASSWARE. Indiana Crystal, fired-on white, gold edges, pink azaleas, green foliage. First issued in 1928. ITEM 11, fruit bowl, 8-1/2", about 2-3/4" deep. ITEM 112, 10" sandwich tray; ITEM 111, cheese and cracker set, large 10" tray with recess for cheese tray, 2-1/4" cheese tray. ITEM 124, cake plate, 10-1/2" diameter, two handled, also called sandwich tray; ITEM 113, footed comport, 10" diameter, 3-1/2" high; ITEM 114, candlesticks, 3-3/4" diameter, 3-3/4" high.

DRESSER SET. Rose pink, also green. Often dresser sets were advertised as two bud vases and one powder box, or two colognes and one puff box. Sets are plain, etched, or decorated. ITEM 84, two 9-1/2" bud vases, 3-3/4" diameter powder box.

THREE PETAL FLORAL AND LEAF CUT. Green, pink, crystal. Three oblong petals, with leaves each side of floral motif. ITEM 91, six dainty green glasses for ices, custards, and other desserts, 4-3/4" high; ITEM 94, set of six plates cut in floral design, advertised as "cool green"; ITEM 93, 8" diameter salad plates, cut in floral design; ITEM 92, bridge set, four tumblers of diamond optic shape, 5" high, handled tray 6-1/2" square.

HAND PAINTED AZALEA GLASSWARE

The ever popular, colorful Azalea pattern here decorates charming pieces of crystal glassware, hand-painted in all its attractiveness on a wide band of white. Gold edges add the final note of richness. A Fruit Bowl and Cake Plate, new with this Catalog, give added variety to the selection.

Dainty set of rose-pink glass, consisting of covered powder box, 3¾ in. in diameter and two graceful bud vases about 9½ in. high. Mlg. wt. 2 lbs.

11

112

111

124

114

113

114

84

91

94

93

92

Plate 13

DOUBLE BRANCH CANDLEHOLDERS. Origin unknown, 1930s. Black, pink. One reeded branch stands higher than the other. Some believe this to be a Heisey variant. ROW I 1 and 3, 5" high, black.

OCTAGON CAKE-SANDWICH TRAY. Lancaster Glass Co., 1926-32. Black, pink, green, topaz, crystal, plain, etched or decorated. ROW I 2, 10-1/2" diameter cake-sandwich tray, black.

DECAGON STYLE. Cambridge, 1926-30s. Black, rose, green, amber, possibly other Cambridge colors. Cup and saucer each have Cambridge trademark. ROW II 1, 7-1/2" plate, black; ROW II 2 and 3, cup and saucer, black.

"S" PATTERN. Westmoreland, late 1920s. Re-issued 1940 to 197-. Black, white opal. Older "S" pattern square plates have earlier Westmoreland trademark. No difference in molds of today from yesterday. ROW II 4, 8" square plate, black.

SNAKE DANCE. L. E. Smith, 1928-32. Cobalt blue, black. Impressed L. E. Smith trade-mark on window box. Girls dancing with snakes and Pan playing pipe is motif. ROW II 5, 7-3/4" window box, sold with or without flower block; ROW IV 5 and 6, 4" high salt-pepper shakers, black, burnished gold lids.

STIPPLED BLOCK. L. E. Smith. 1920s-early 1930s. Black, cobalt blue. Creamers, sugars have been verified in this pattern. ROW III 1, creamer, black.

HORSE BOOKEND. New Martinsville, 1930s. Black, crystal. Scarce in black. New Martinsville made several horse items in their novelty line. ROW III 2, rearing horse bookends, 8-1/2" high.

SMITH-515 LINE. L. E. Smith, late 1920s-early 1930s. Black, cobalt blue. Similar to Fenton's eight-spine pillow mold, same period. ROW III 3, black 7" diameter, footed, cupped bowl.

CRIMPED TOP VASE. L. E. Smith, late 1920s-early 1930s. Black, cobalt blue. Number of crimps identify the vase shapes. ROW III 4, black 6-crimp vase, 5" high.

GREENSBURG CANDLEHOLDER. Greensburg. 1928-36. Black, green, pink, opal, amber. Cataloged as No. 1402. ROW IV 1 and 3, No. 1402 three leg candleholder, black.

ROLLED RIM CONSOLE BOWL. Origin unknown, late 1920s. Most factories made rolled rim bowls. Catalog illustrations appear identical. They vary in weight, thickness, etc. ROW IV 2, 11" console bowl, 2-1/4" high, black.

SMALL JAM COMPORT. Black, 1920s. Floral pattern inside bowl. Origin unknown, possibly Canton Glass Co. ROW IV 4, black 2-1/2" high.

Plate 14

LAMPS. The lamps shown are of the 1920 to 1930 period. They were advertised in household catalogs, sold through the five-and-dime stores, and used in the wholesale trade for promotional wares. By 1926 matching glass shades were waning in popularity and the glasshouses returned for the most part to non-glass shades.

ROW I 1, crystal 14" electric lamp, green fired over crystal glass shade, square base. ROW I 2, English Hobnail, No. 555, Westmoreland oil lamp, green. Made in electric or gas, green, crystal, white opal, roselin. Today in crystal and white opal ware. ROW I 3, *Colonial Block* and *Punty No. 185* electric lamp. Westmoreland. Electric or oil in crystal, green, roselin and white opal. 12-1/4" high.

ROW II 1, *Debutante* electric, 9-1/2" high, billowing skirt, fired-on blue, pink or white over crystal glass. ROW II 2, *Dancing Girl* electric lamp, U.S. Glass, advertised with glass shade or non-glass shade, fired-on blue, pink or white on crystal glass. ROW II 3, five scotties-in-a-basket, electric lamp, 7" high without shade. Fired-on blue, pink, white over crystal glass.

ROW II 4 and 5, dancers electric lamps, crystal and crystal frost, 7-1/2" high, without shade, hole in base for electric fixture attachment. ROW III 1, crystal lamp, green fired center shaft to subdue fixture in shaft, round base, 9" high. ROW III 2, English Hobnail electric sewing lamp No. 555. Crystal, white opal, green and roselin. 9-1/2" high, shown in crystal. ROW III 3, crystal fish electric lamp, solid fish, hollow base, 5-3/4" high, 8" long. ROW III 4, crystal two handled electric lamp, round ripple base, 8-3/4" high, parchment shade. ROW III 5, opaline tiered base electric lamp, pull chain, 10" high, two columns of decorative black floral design.

ROW I 4, Martele line, 1926-37. Consolidated Lamp & Glass Co. All vases advertised as lamp bases also. A fixture and a parchment shade transformed any vase to a lamp. Martele line has a hand-wrought appearance in semi-transparent finish, advertised as the nearest in appearance to the Lalique French glass. Martele is the type of finish, not the pattern name. Shown is *Dogwood* pattern in French crystal. 1931 catalog lists colors of honey, lilac, amethyst, sepia, French crystal, russet, rose and jade.

Plate 15

SATIN IRIDESCENT, called stretch glass by today's collectors, is a satin and crackle mineral finish applied to assorted glass blanks. Lustre glassware is shiny, not a satin crackle. Lustre glass is very slick to touch. Jade iridescents are very rare, being opaque jade glass with iridescent crizzle applied. LANCASTER GLASS COMPANY were decorators of iridescent, painted, etched and cut lines, as well as producers of blanks for other firms. This company, no longer in existence, was a subsidiary of Hocking Glass Company from around 1910 until it no longer existed in the late 1930s. WESTMORELAND made only lustre ware, no satin iridescent stretch or jade iridescent. IMPERIAL manufactured Imperial Jewels, an art glass not shown here, satin iridescent and lustre glassware. FENTON made satin iridescent, called its Florentine Line at the factory, and lustre.

1 and 3. EGYPTIAN SUGAR AND CREAMER. 1924. Westmoreland. Crystal with marigold lustre bowl, or Westmoreland transparent colors with marigold lustre bowl. Advertisements referred to this as "gold linings, iridescent lustre surface." Egyptian is a Westmoreland advertising name. Set sold for 18 cents wholesale, 49 cents retail in 1929. 1, marigold lustre on clear base glass; 3, marigold lustre bowl over teal green, transparent base glass.

2. ORANGE BOWL. origin unknown, 1922. The base color is a deep green like that made by both H. Northwood and Diamond Glass.

4. COLONIAL. Imperial. Rubigold. Imperial advertisements referred to this wide paneled (not optic) pattern as Colonial. The lid is product of Fenton.

5. CONE OPTIC candy jar base or open bonbon. Sold as both. This is Fenton's lustre color, marigold lustre. This is a lustre item, not a satin iridescent. Fenton's mold No. 736 was produced in 1921-28 in assorted jade opaque colors, lustres, and their Florentine treatment.

6. CUPPED NUT BOWL. The cupped bowl is a product of either Imperial or Fenton as both made the marigold lustre and both made cupped nut bowls. They appear identical in catalogs. Bowl is 4-3/4" on a collar base.

7. LANCASTER BLUE FLORAL candy jar. 1929. Lancaster Glass Co. Hand painted blue enamel flowers and leaves adorn the lid. Light crystal ice over crystal glass, except that finial and foot have no crizzle.

8. TRUMPET. 4-1/2" vase, ice green over green base glass. Origin unknown.

9. IMPERIAL'S INSIDE WIDE PANEL. Nuruby bowl with black painted foot, open bonbon.

10. MUFFIN DISH. Lancaster. Dishes with turned up sides advertised as muffin dishes. Lightly crizzled in crystal ice (white) over transparent crystal glass.

11. LANCASTER BLUE FLORAL Console Bowl. 1929. 11-1/4" diameter, 2-3/4" high. Hand painted blue enameled flowers, same as item 7. Crystal ice.

12. TALL COMPOTE. Lancaster. 9" high, heavily iced rubigold.

Photography of this plate by Foley Studio, Bellevue, Wa. Items 5, 9, 11, 4, 6, courtesy Cheryl Leaf Antiques, Bellingham, Wa.

Plate 16

AURORA IRIDESCENT "STRETCH" Glass. 1925-27. U.S. Glass Company. Canary ice, Tiffin blue ice, crystal ice (frosty white), rose ice; opaque iridescent colors Nile green and Tiffin blue. Each pattern shown has been named by U.S. Glass in their trade journal advertisements. Aurora is the name given to satin and crackle iridescent tints. This glass is depression era, not necessarily depression glass. Names as they appear below are U.S. Glass official names.

1. CUMULA. 4-1/4" footed comport, canary ice. The Cumula pattern has four or six panel sets, one panel raised; the other two, one each side, are indented; a slight scallop is created where the panels meet the rim of the bowl, but not as pronounced as in their *Chatham* pattern.

2. FLARED LILY VASE. 11-1/2" high. Canary ice. The finish is very smooth.

3. BANDED AURORA fruit comport (cover). Crystal ice. 6-1/4" high. 8-1/8" rim diameter. If the *Aurora* pattern is decorated with black bands it is referred to as banded. Aurora is plain without pattern except for the round ball and thin flat wafer on the stem, identical to that of the *Cumula*.

4 and 10. FLORENTINE salad bowl. No. 4 as shown is opaque Nile green; 10 is semi-transparent Tiffin blue ice. The Florentine shape, as named by U.S. Glass, is another "panel" piece. It has six sets of panels; at the rim the panel rim edge is scooped out in a low dip. No. 4 is an opaque jade glass with the light crystal ice crizzled over the inside lustrous surface. No. 10 of Tiffin blue is a very light powdery blue, unlike any other blue in the satin iridescent lines made by the various companies.

5. CUMULA salad bowl. Canary ice. 10-1/2" diameter bowl flares out gently, showing the units of panels described in No. 1. Base rim is polished, the "dope" heavily applied. *Courtesy Mr. and Mrs. Melvyn Stimson, Bellevue, Wa.*

6. CUMULA small comport. 5" high, 5-1/2" flared rim diameter. Crystal ice.

7. CHATHAM rolled down console bowl. The *Chatham* panels are clearly shown in this bowl. The indented panels border each side of the raised panel, with a large rim scallop between the panels. 10-1/2" bowl is rose ice. *Courtesy Cheryl Leaf Antiques, Bellingham, Wa.*

8. OLD LEEDSWARE bowl. Crystal ice. 10-3/4" diameter. Polished rim. Crystal ices have shimmering pink, blue highlights, most often mistaken for Imperial Jewels. In the olden days, ribbons of your favorite color were run in and out between the openwork. Also made in non-iridescents, opaques, and satin finishes.

9. CUMULA flared comport. Tiffin blue ice. 6-1/2" diameter, 5" high. Foot is always round, not scalloped as in the *Chatham* pattern. *Courtesy Cheryl Leaf Antiques, Bellingham, Wa.*

Photography of this plate by Foley Studio, Bellevue, Wa.

Plate 17

MITRE CUT CREAMER. ROW I 1. Late 1920s-early 1930s. Pink, aqua-green, green and crystal. Berry cream and sugar only verified to date.

OPTIC FLUTE AND BUZZSAW. ROW I 2. Imperial Glass Co., 1930s. Crystal. A small line of 20 or more items issued in occasional pieces. Shown is oval celery dish.

FLUTED COLONIAL. ROW I 3. Indiana Glass Co. Three legs. Another similar design with four legs issued by another company same period. Indiana made this berry sugar in pink, green, crystal, amber and Indiana Blue.

WESTMORELAND NO. 1211. ROW I 4. Decorating concern unknown. 6-1/2" handled jelly dish. Cut in floral and three-spray leaf motif. Pink, green, crystal.

13-BALL GRAPE Pattern. Standard Glass Mfg. Co., 1925-30. Green, rose, crystal, topaz. Grape pattern cuts will have numerous balls and ball arrangement in the grape. Count formation when assembling sets. Shown is *Standard Cut 236*. ROW II 1, 80 oz. jug, green; ROW II 2, 12 oz. ice tea, 5" high; ROW II 3, green 5 oz. juice, 3-7/8" high.

CRACKLE CARNIVAL. Water set, berry bowl set and open and covered jars made in marigold lustre. ROW II 4, candy jar, no lid, sold both ways; ROW II 5, footed cone tumbler 4-3/4" high; ROW II 6, jug, 8" high.

SAILS. Hazel Atlas 1938. Cobalt blue. Cocktail shaker with or without strainer, assorted glasses, and plates. ROW III 1, *Sails* cocktail shaker; ROW III 2, juice tumbler.

WILD WEST water set. Crystal, green. Origin unknown. 1930 period. Buffalo, mountains and assorted "wild west" animals lightly embossed. ROW III 3, Wild West crystal jug, ice guard; ROW III 4, amber 15 oz. iced tea tumbler; ROW III 5, 12 oz. tumbler, lighter amber than No. 4 tumbler.

DUNBAR BALL CUTTING. ROW III 6. Early 1930. Green, crystal. 5-ball pattern. Jug stands 9-1/4" high, sold with or without cover.

SCALLOPED FLUTE JUG. ROW IV 1. Aqua. Sold in Woolworth stores in late 1920s. Heavy, 8" high.

VERTICAL RIB-OPTIC FLUTE pitcher. ROW IV 2. Late 1920s. Two patterns in one jug. Stands 8-1/4" high. Green and crystal.

WORLD ROUND Jug. ROW IV 3. Advertised in pink, crystal, green. Federal. 1930s.

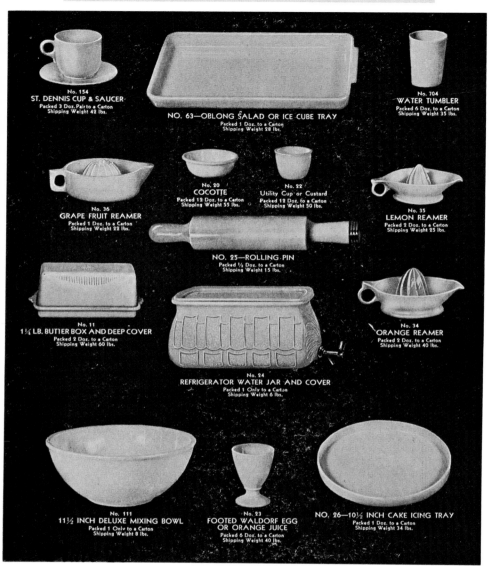

No. 154
ST. DENNIS CUP & SAUCER
Packed 3 Doz. Pair to a Carton
Shipping Weight 42 lbs.

NO. 63—OBLONG SALAD OR ICE CUBE TRAY
Packed 1 Doz. to a Carton
Shipping Weight 28 lbs.

No. 704
WATER TUMBLER
Packed 6 Doz. to a Carton
Shipping Weight 35 lbs.

No. 36
GRAPE FRUIT REAMER
Packed 1 Doz. to a Carton
Shipping Weight 22 lbs.

No. 20
COCOTTE
Packed 12 Doz. to a Carton
Shipping Weight 55 lbs.

No. 22
Utility Cup or Custard
Packed 12 Doz. to a Carton
Shipping Weight 50 lbs.

No. 35
LEMON REAMER
Packed 2 Doz. to a Carton
Shipping Weight 25 lbs.

NO. 25—ROLLING PIN
Packed ½ Doz. to a Carton
Shipping Weight 15 lbs.

No. 11
1¼ LB. BUTTER BOX AND DEEP COVER
Packed 2 Doz. to a Carton
Shipping Weight 60 lbs.

No. 24
REFRIGERATOR WATER JAR AND COVER
Packed 1 Only to a Carton
Shipping Weight 6 lbs.

No. 34
ORANGE REAMER
Packed 2 Doz. to a Carton
Shipping Weight 40 lbs.

No. 111
11½ INCH DELUXE MIXING BOWL
Packed 1 Only to a Carton
Shipping Weight 8 lbs.

No. 23
FOOTED WALDORF EGG OR ORANGE JUICE
Packed 6 Doz. to a Carton
Shipping Weight 40 lbs.

NO. 26—10½ INCH CAKE ICING TRAY
Packed 1 Doz. to a Carton
Shipping Weight 34 lbs.

McKEE GLASS COMPANY, 1930-40. Skokie green was the most prominent color made in the matched pieces of refrigerator and kitchen ware. Seville yellow and Chalaine blue were made in smaller quantities. A few pieces were made in black and are very high in value today. The unusual items on Plate 18 are the refrigerator water jug with flat cover, the rolling pin, and the 1-1/4 lb. butter box. None of the items shown on Plate 18 are in abundance today. The utility items shown on Plate 19 are more common and can be found with little difficulty. Not shown in this line is a round salt box with metal hinge cover, quart batter jug and assorted box storage containers, round, square and oblong.

McKEE DELUXE

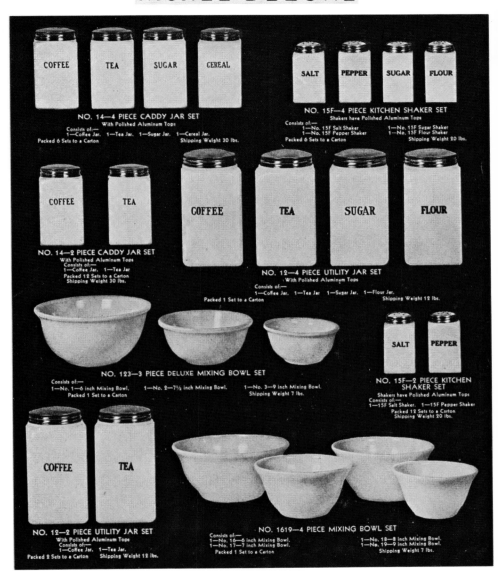

COFFEE TEA SUGAR CEREAL

NO. 14—4 PIECE CADDY JAR SET
With Polished Aluminum Tops
Consists of:—
1—Coffee Jar. 1—Tea Jar. 1—Sugar Jar. 1—Cereal Jar.
Packed 6 Sets to a Carton Shipping Weight 30 lbs.

SALT PEPPER SUGAR FLOUR

NO. 15F—4 PIECE KITCHEN SHAKER SET
Shakers have Polished Aluminum Tops
Consists of:—
1—No. 15F Salt Shaker 1—No. 15F Sugar Shaker
1—No. 15F Pepper Shaker 1—No. 15F Flour Shaker
Packed 6 Sets to a Carton Shipping Weight 20 lbs.

COFFEE TEA

NO. 14—2 PIECE CADDY JAR SET
With Polished Aluminum Tops
Consists of:—
1—Coffee Jar. 1—Tea Jar
Packed 12 Sets to a Carton
Shipping Weight 30 lbs.

COFFEE TEA SUGAR FLOUR

NO. 12—4 PIECE UTILITY JAR SET
With Polished Aluminum Tops
Consists of:—
1—Coffee Jar. 1—Tea Jar. 1—Sugar Jar. 1—Flour Jar.
Packed 1 Set to a Carton Shipping Weight 12 lbs.

NO. 123—3 PIECE DELUXE MIXING BOWL SET
Consists of:—
1—No. 1—6 inch Mixing Bowl. 1—No. 2—7½ inch Mixing Bowl. 1—No. 3—9 inch Mixing Bowl.
Packed 1 Set to a Carton Shipping Weight 7 lbs.

SALT PEPPER

NO. 15F—2 PIECE KITCHEN SHAKER SET
Shakers have Polished Aluminum Tops
Consists of:—
1—15F Salt Shaker. 1—15F Pepper Shaker
Packed 12 Sets to a Carton
Shipping Weight 20 lbs.

COFFEE TEA

NO. 12—2 PIECE UTILITY JAR SET
With Polished Aluminum Tops
Consists of:—
1—Coffee Jar. 1—Tea Jar.
Packed 2 Sets to a Carton Shipping Weight 12 lbs.

NO. 1619—4 PIECE MIXING BOWL SET
Consists of:—
1—No. 16—6 inch Mixing Bowl. 1—No. 18—8 inch Mixing Bowl.
1—No. 17—7 inch Mixing Bowl. 1—No. 19—9 inch Mixing Bowl.
Packed 1 Set to a Carton Shipping Weight 7 lbs.

Plate 19

GOLD ENCRUSTED No. 2 LINE.
ROSE PINK COLOR.
ROUND SHAPES.

No. 153. 12 inch Console Bowl, Flanged

No. 151. Footed May. Comport and Plate with

No. 100. 1 pound Covered Candy Jar Optic

No. 154. 10 inch Comport, Flat Edge

No. 153. 4 inch Roll Edge Candlestick Low.

No. 153. 4 inch Roll Edge Candlestick

No. 153. 11½ inch Center Bowl, Roll Edge

No. 153. 11 inch Round Covered Cheese Box and Cracker Plate

No. 151. 11 inch Handled Lunch Plate

Plate 20

McKEE GLASS COMPANY. 1925. Green or rose-pink. This is the gold encrusted No. 2 line. The *Wreath Medallion* design is heavily encrusted on round blanks. The line is larger than this 1925 brochure illustrates. The rose-pink color has been issued by McKee since 1904, definitely a leader in colored glassware. The popular colors during the depression period were all made at the McKee plant—amethyst, green, rose-pink, amber, topaz, black, crystal, ruby, blue, amberina; and the jade colors—jade green, poudre blue, lime green ivory, French ivory, and others.

GOLD ENCRUSTED No. 3 LINE.
ROSE PINK COLOR.
OCTAGON SHAPES.

No. 155. 12 inch Console Bowl, Flanged

No. 155. Candy Jar and Cover

No. 155. Footed May. Comport and Plate with Ladle

No. 155. 10 inch Comport, Flat Edge

No. 200. Candlestick, Low

No. 155. 11½ inch Center Bowl, Roll Edge

No. 200. Candlestick, Low

11 inch Covered Cheese Box and Cracker Plate

No. 155. 11 inch Handled Lunch Plate

Plate 21

McKEE GLASS COMPANY. 1925. Rose pink or green. This is the encrusted No. 3 line. The No. 3 line was decorated on octagon transparent blanks. The line is somewhat larger than illustrated here. This is not a dinnerware but a parlor or occasional line for the coffee or console table. The gold encrusted wares were popular from 1920 to 1930.

This attractive jade green glassware is one of the most successful lines brought out. The sof
table decoration. Shipped direct from factory

Thin blown glassware.
6270 Goblets. Tall Sherbets. Footed Tumblers. Coasters.

6253 Handled Candlesticks.

6246 Flower Holder. 2½ in. / 3½ in.   6248 8½ in. Bowl and Standard.   6238 7½ in. Bowl and Standard.

6252 Candlesticks, 8¾ in. hig

6254 8½ in. Plate.   6285 6¾ in. Bon Bon.   625 7½ in. Comport.

6256 8½ in. Bowl and Standard.

624 13 in. Bowl and Standard and 3½ in. Flower Block.

6257 11 in. Bowl and Standard.

6265 Console Set with 3½ in. Flow Does not include candles or fl

6251 Console Set. Does not include candles or fruit.

62 10½ in. Bowl and Standard.

6258 1 lb. Candy Jar.   6259 ½ lb.

Plate 22

CARSON PIRIE SCOTT FLYER from the late 1920s-early 1930s. The Fenton Art Glass Company made special order items and colors distributed through the wholesale branch of Carson Pirie Scott & Co., Chicago, Ill., in their glassware division. These special order items were from Fenton's regular molds, used by Fenton in their semi-translucent jade colors and their Florentine iridescent colors. These are referred to as stretch glass today.

ught out.   The soft coloring of the various pieces give it complete harmony with any
direct from factory, at factory prices.

626   Cheese and Cracker Plate.

6261   Sandwich Plate.

6262   7½ in. Bon Bon.

6263   7 in. Comport.

6264   Mayonnaise and Plate.

6255   Candlesticks.

Candlesticks, 8¾ in. high.

6289   9½ in. Bowl and Standard.

6245   Handle Candlestick.

6247   8½ in. Comport.

6291   Sweetmeat

6243   11½ in. Footed Bowl.

6260   10 in. Bowl and Standard.

nsole Set with 3½ in. Flower Block.
oes not include candles or flowers.

6244   Bowl and Standard.

6289   ½ lb.

6283   Bon Bon.

6249   Console Set.   Does not include candles or fruit.

CARSON PIRIE SCOTT & CO.
CHICAGO
Colored Glass Division

Plate 23

Only the transparent jade green color illustrated here was sold to Carson
Pirie Scott. Mr. Fenton corroborates that they made glassware for this
concern, but exactly what items is unknown. This two-page illustrated flyer is
an excellent guide for the collectors attempting to identify their glassware.
Regardless of the color, the line numbers stated in the flyer will aid the
collector in identifying the mold shape.

McKEE GLASS COMPANY., JEANNETTE, PA.

No. 150 Colored Light Cut Salad Plates. Any Pattern can be furnished in the
Sea Green, Amber, Blue or Canary Color. Two sizes of Plates, 7½ inch and 8½ inch.

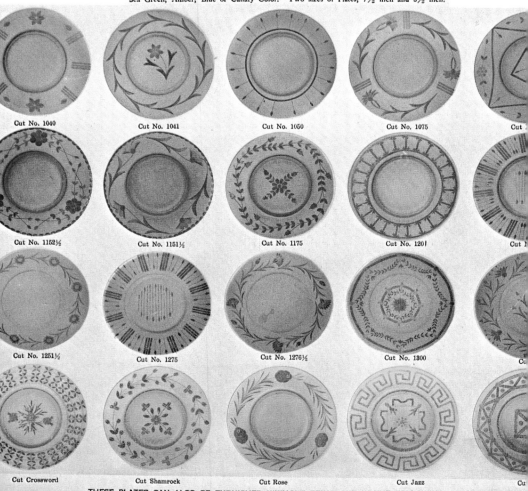

Cut No. 1040 Cut No. 1041 Cut No. 1050 Cut No. 1075 Cut

Cut No. 1152½ Cut No. 1151½ Cut No. 1175 Cut No. 1201 Cut

Cut No. 1251½ Cut No. 1275 Cut No. 1276½ Cut No. 1300 Cu

Cut Crossword Cut Shamrock Cut Rose Cut Jazz Cu

THESE PLATES CAN ALSO BE FURNISHED WITHOUT BEING CUT IN THE FOLLOWING COLORS,
SEA GREEN, AMBER, BLUE, CANARY AND AMETHYST.

Plate 24

McKEE GLASS COMPANY. 1925-30. Sea green, amethyst, amber, blue, canary. Cut on colored blanks, except for amethyst. Salad plates came in 7-1/2" and 8-1/2" sizes. Low sherbets were also made for dessert sets. Twenty different cuts are illustrated. Most items issued by glass companies were not named and were known only by line numbers. For identification purposes, these patterns can be referred to by number as listed on the brochure, i.e., McKee Cut No. 1040. For the mail-order collector especially, line numbers are an easy identification when attempting to communicate pattern descriptions. Other items besides salad and dessert sets were cut in all of the cut patterns shown here.